Magnetism

LEON GRAY

 Gareth Stevens
Publishing

Please visit our website, www.garethstevens.com. For a free color catalog of all our high-quality books, call toll free 1-800-542-2595 or fax 1-877-542-2596.

Library of Congress Cataloging-in-Publication Data

Gray, Leon.
Magnetism / by Leon Gray.
   p. cm. — (Physical science)
Includes index.
ISBN 978-1-4339-9517-0 (pbk.)
ISBN 978-1-4339-9518-7 (6-pack)
ISBN 978-1-4339-9516-3 (library binding)
1. Magnetism — Juvenile literature. I. Gray, Leon, 1974-. II. Title.
QC753.7 G73 2014
538—d23

First Edition

Published in 2014 by
Gareth Stevens Publishing
111 East 14th Street, Suite 349
New York, NY 10003

Produced by Calcium, www.calciumcreative.co.uk
Designed by Simon Borrough
Edited by Sarah Eason and Jennifer Sanderson

Pic credits: Cover: Shutterstock: Worradirek. Inside: Dreamstime: Andres Rodriguez 33, 38t, Candybox Images 4, Ckellyphoto 38b, Cyoginan 44, Diego Vito Cervo 5, Dreamstimepoint 42, Evgeny Karandaev 13, Jarp3 18, Kiyagrafica 36, Miguel Castro 1, 23, Parkinsonsniper 41, Retro77 22, R. Gino Santa Maria 16, Ron Chapple 9, Stepan Popov 37, Yury Shirokov 32; NASA 17, 45; Shutterstock: Alexandre17 25, Anaken2012 24, Design56 3, 12, Dubassy 29, Iofoto 11, Isaravut 30, Fzd.it 6, MilanB 14, 15, 21, Mitzy 7, Monkey Business Images 35, Morphart Creation 26, Nicku 28, 31, REDAV 40, Terry Alexander 27, TFoxFoto 8, Zigzag Mountain Art; Wikimedia Commons: Bin im Garten 19, Ryan Somma 10, Torkild Retvedt 43.

Printed in the United States of America

CPSIA compliance information: Batch #CS13GS: For further information contact Gareth Stevens, New York, New York at 1-800-542-2595.

Contents

Magnificent Magnetism

Magnetism has puzzled people for thousands of years. Magnets are all around us, from magnetic rocks found beneath Earth's surface to the magnets inside everyday household appliances. Even Earth itself is a giant magnet!

Push and Pull

Magnetism is the force that pushes and pulls on some objects, forcing them apart or dragging them together. Most materials are magnetic, but you can detect magnetism only in certain materials, especially metals such as iron and nickel.

Fundamental Forces

No one really knows what causes magnetism. Scientists think that the movement of tiny particles, called electrons, inside atoms causes magnetism. These same particles create electricity, and scientists know that electricity and magnetism are closely related.

Tiny magnets inside headphones convert the electrical signals from a music player into the music you can hear.

In fact, electricity and magnetism are one and the same force, called electromagnetism. Electromagnetism is one of the fundamental forces of nature.

Useful Magnetism

In the late nineteenth century, scientists found the link between electricity and magnetism. They invented machines called generators, which use magnets to make electricity to heat and light homes. Later, they invented electric motors, which use electricity and magnets to drive the moving parts of machines. Today, most household appliances and vehicles contain magnets. Every time you watch television, fly in an airplane, or surf the Internet, you are relying on magnetism to work for you.

Hikers use compasses to stay on the right track. The compass needle always points to magnetic north.

LIFE WITHOUT MAGNETISM

Imagine what life would be like without magnetism. There would be no easily available electricity for power, no motors to drive machines and vehicles, such as computers and cars. We also would not have compasses to find our way when we are lost.

Chapter One

What Is Magnetism?

Magnetism is a natural form of energy that has been around since the beginning of the universe. People use magnets all the time—from the magnets in science laboratories and the needle of a compass to the magnets on refrigerator doors. Other magnets are hidden away inside machines to make them work.

World of Atoms

Everything in the universe is made up of tiny particles called atoms. In turn, atoms consist of smaller particles called protons, neutrons, and electrons. Protons and neutrons cluster together in the dense center, or nucleus, of an atom. Protons have a positive electric charge, while neutrons have no electric charge. Electrons have a negative electric charge, which balances the positive charge of the protons to make an atom electrically neutral.

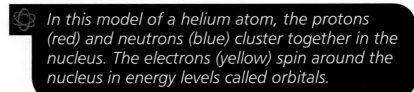

In this model of a helium atom, the protons (red) and neutrons (blue) cluster together in the nucleus. The electrons (yellow) spin around the nucleus in energy levels called orbitals.

In a Spin

Scientists like to think of the electrons as planets, which spin in orbit around the sun (the nucleus). In an atom, the electrons spin around the nucleus in a series of energy levels called orbitals. Electrons spin around the nucleus in pairs, but in opposite directions—one up and one down. It is the up-and-down spinning movement of electrons that causes magnetism.

Magnetic Moment

In most atoms, electrons spin around in opposite directions so that the magnetism cancels out. In naturally magnetic materials, such as iron and nickel, the atoms contain unpaired electrons. This creates a "magnetic moment," which gives the material its magnetic effect.

An iron bar can be magnetized by rubbing it with a magnet. The rubbing spins the electrons like a basketball player spins a basketball.

Permanent and Temporary Magnets

Some magnets are called permanent magnets. They keep their magnetism for a long time. Others are called temporary magnets, which means they keep their magnetism for a short time before it disappears.

Permanent Magnets

Magnets are materials that produce magnetic force fields that attract other magnetic materials. Permanent magnets create a magnetic force field all the time and keep their magnetism forever.

Temporary Magnets

Materials that create a magnetic force field for a short time only are temporary magnets. Any object that is attracted to a magnet becomes a temporary magnet. This magnetism disappears when the permanent magnet is removed. Other materials become temporary magnets when an electric current flows through them.

An electromagnet in a junkyard is a temporary magnet.

SUPER SCIENCE FACT

Electromagnets are temporary magnets. They produce magnetic fields when an electrical current runs through them. The magnetic field disappears when the current stops (see Chapter Five).

Hard and Soft

The materials used to make permanent magnets are called hard magnetic materials. For this reason, permanent magnets are sometimes called hard magnets. Soft magnetic materials are used to make temporary, or soft magnets.

Strong and Weak

Some magnets are much stronger than other magnets. Strong magnets create more magnetic force than weak magnets. This is because the atoms of these materials have more unpaired electrons, which creates a stronger magnetic moment. The bar magnets and horseshoe magnets that you find in a science laboratory are examples of strong magnets.

This horseshoe magnet is attracting steel screws. Horseshoe magnets are strong magnets.

Magnetic Materials

Magnets will attract any magnetic material. The magnet's force field pulls on the other magnetic material. This pulling force makes the magnetic material stick to the magnet.

Magnetic Rock
A type of rock called lodestone is a permanent magnet. It contains an iron ore called magnetite. This material is the strongest of all naturally occurring magnetic materials.

Metal Magnets
Some metals, such as cobalt, iron, and nickel are permanent magnets. Many metal alloys (mixtures of metals) are also permanent magnets. Steel is a magnetic material. This alloy is made from iron, carbon, and other metals such as chromium, nickel, and tungsten.

Modern Magnets
Today, most magnets are made from man-made magnetic materials to create magnets of different strengths.
• Ceramic magnets contain iron oxide (iron mixed with oxygen) combined with a ceramic material. Ceramic magnets are weak and are used to make fridge magnets.

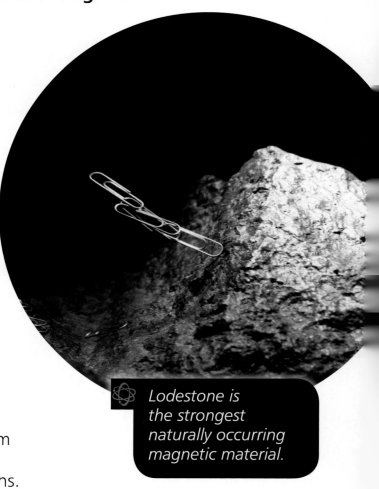

Lodestone is the strongest naturally occurring magnetic material.

- Alnico magnets consist of the metals aluminum, nickel, and cobalt. These common man-made magnets are weaker than permanent magnets but stronger than ceramic magnets.
- Rare-earth magnets are made from a group of rare metals, including neodymium and samarium, mixed with other materials. They are much stronger than ceramic and alnico magnets, but they are very expensive because rare-earth metals are uncommon.
- Scientists have recently made plastic magnets in laboratories. These magnets are soft and bendable because the magnetic material is mixed with plastics. However, they are not very strong and usually work only at low temperatures.

Fridge magnets stick to the metal door of a refrigerator.

LIFE WITHOUT ALLOYS

Alloys are very important as magnetic materials, but also have other uses such as in industry. Alloys combine the properties of all the metals from which they are made, for example, making the alloy lighter, stronger, or more flexible depending on which metals are in them.

Chapter Two

How Magnetism Works

Magnetism is an invisible force, but you can feel the effects of two magnets when they push and pull on each other. Although magnets have always existed, until recently no one could explain how they worked.

Magnetic Poles

Every magnet has two parts with the greatest pulling power. Called poles, these parts are the places where the magnetic force seems strongest. One is called the north pole, and the other is the south pole.

A horseshoe magnet is much stronger than a simple bar magnet because the poles are closer together.

North and South

The poles of a magnet are called the north and south pole because they are attracted to Earth's natural magnetism (see pages 16–17). If you tie a piece of thread around a bar magnet and let it hang freely in the air, the magnet will align itself so that the north pole points to Earth's North Pole. For this reason, the north pole is often called the "north-seeking" pole. Similarly, the magnet's south pole will point to Earth's South Pole. It is called the "south-seeking" pole.

 The engine and cars of this toy train connect to each other using small magnets.

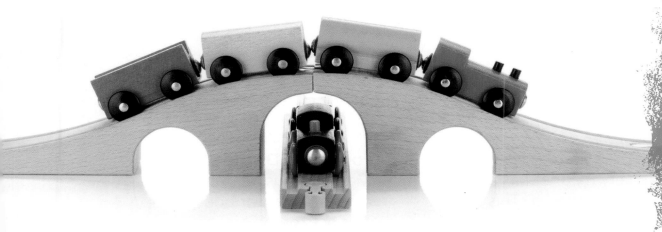

Attraction and Repulsion

Magnets push and pull on each other according to a very simple rule. This rule states that like poles repel (push against) each other, while unlike poles attract (pull toward) each other. So when two north poles are brought together, the magnets push apart. The same thing happens when two south poles are brought together. When the north pole of one magnet is brought near the south pole of another magnet, the two magnets attract each other strongly and move closer together.

Magnetic Field

Magnets do not have to touch to push and pull each other because magnetism acts at a distance. The magnetic effects occur in an area called the magnetic field.

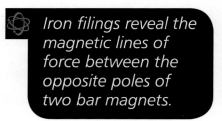

Iron filings reveal the magnetic lines of force between the opposite poles of two bar magnets.

Force Field

Every magnet has a magnetic field around it. This is the space around a magnet in which the magnet can attract other magnetic materials. If the material is outside this invisible force field, the magnet cannot attract it.

Force at a Distance

Magnetism is an example of a noncontact, or body, force. This acts on objects through an invisible force field that pushes and pulls on magnetic materials. The force field is strongest around the poles of the magnet and gets weaker the farther away from the magnet you are.

Forces make objects move by pushing and pulling on them. Most forces are contact forces that act on objects when they touch each other. Magnetism is a noncontact force because magnets can push and pull on other magnets without touching them. Other examples of noncontact forces include electricity and gravity.

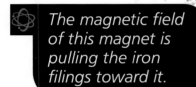

The magnetic field of this magnet is pulling the iron filings toward it.

Lines of Force

The magnetic field of a magnet is invisible, but you can imagine it as a series of lines of magnetic force. These lines of force extend from the north pole to the south pole of the same magnet, or the south pole of another nearby magnet. You can actually see these lines of force if you sprinkle iron filings around a bar magnet. The magnetic field pulls the iron filings into lines that represent the lines of magnetic force.

Earth's Magnetic Field

 Scientists believe that geese and other migratory birds find their way by sensing Earth's magnetic field.

Earth is a giant magnet. Deep inside Earth is a core of molten iron, which creates a vast magnetic field around the planet. This magnetic field, called the magnetosphere, extends more than 35,000 miles (56,000 km) into space.

Natural Magnetism

Earth's natural magnetic field is not very strong. At the surface of Earth, a small bar magnet is hundreds of times stronger than Earth's magnetic field. But Earth's magnetism is strong enough to make all magnets align themselves to Earth's magnetic field.

North and South

The north pole of any magnet always points toward Earth's magnetic north pole. The south pole of a magnet will always point toward Earth's magnetic south pole on the opposite side of the planet. A compass needle is a magnet, so its north pole points toward Earth's magnetic north pole to help people find their way (see pages 22–23).

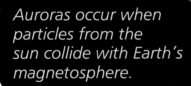

Auroras occur when particles from the sun collide with Earth's magnetosphere.

The Magnetosphere

Earth's magnetic field may be very weak, but it does the important job of stopping damaging solar particles from the sun from hitting Earth. When these solar particles hit the magnetosphere, especially around Earth's North and South Poles, they create colorful light displays in the sky. These are called auroras.

SUPER SCIENCE FACT

Earth's magnetic field is upside down. When you hang a bar magnet by a thread, the magnet always aligns itself with its north pole pointing toward the North Pole. But we know that like poles repel each other, so the North Pole is actually the planet's south magnetic pole.

Chapter Three

Making Magnets

People have been making magnets for thousands of years, probably without even knowing it. Chinese people found they could magnetize a piece of iron by rubbing it with lodestone—a naturally occurring magnetic material. This is called magnetic induction.

In the Beginning

Although naturally occurring magnets have been around since ancient times, people could not understand magnetism. Eventually, people found out how to make magnets and started to unlock the secrets of this mysterious force.

Greek Ideas

The ancient Greeks were the first people to try and understand magnetism. They came up with all sorts of stories to explain it. One story tells of a Greek shepherd, named Magnes, who discovered magnetism when the soles of his shoes stuck to a mountain.

According to one legend, a shepherd discovered magnetism when an iron tack in his shoe stuck to magnetic rocks.

Magnes thought that the rocks in the mountain contained a "soul" that was pulling his body. In fact, the magnetic rock lodestone was probably attracting the iron nails in his shoes, which caused the strange pulling power of the mountain.

 This Chinese compass was built in the 1800s. The compass needle sits in the middle of a larger circle, which contains information about the time of day and the weather.

SUPER SCIENCE FACT

One of the earliest European scientists to study magnetism was a Frenchman named Petrus Peregrinus of Maricourt. When he tried to separate the poles of a single magnet by cutting it in half, he was amazed to find that each half became a brand-new magnet!

Myths and Magic

The Greeks were smart scientists, but they could not figure out magnetism. In fact, for the next 1,000 years no one made any real progress. During these "dark ages," myths and magic ruled over science. People came up with many different stories about magnets. For example, people used them as a cure for depression by holding them against their heads.

Magnetic Induction

Magnets attract other magnetic materials in a process called magnetic induction. No one knows for sure exactly how this works, but scientists think it is most likely due to the effect spinning electrons have on the atoms that make up a magnetic material.

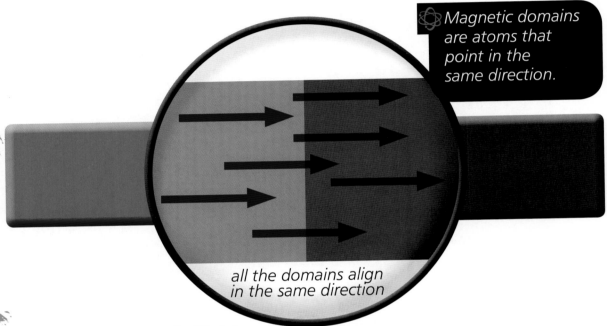

Magnetic domains are atoms that point in the same direction.

all the domains align in the same direction

Creating a Magnetic Field

In the atoms of most materials, the electrons spin around the nucleus in pairs. Since the electrons spin in opposite directions, this cancels out any effect the electrons might have on the material. In permanent magnets, such as a bar of iron, the atoms contain electrons that spin around on their own (see pages 6–7). This causes a magnetic moment to create a magnetic field.

Magnetic Domains

Scientists think that magnetic materials consist of groups of atoms, called domains, which act as individual magnets. All the unpaired spinning electrons produce a magnetic moment that forces the domains to line up along the lines of magnetic force. This creates the magnetic field around a magnet.

These pins become temporary magnets when they are attracted to the red end (north pole) of the bar magnet.

Scientists think that temporary magnets have domains that can easily turn. When a magnet is brought near them, the domains turn to line up with the magnetic lines of force. When the magnet is taken away again, they turn back to their random order. In permanent magnets, it takes much more force to turn the domains. When the magnet is taken away again, the domains are more likely to stay where they are.

Magnetic Attraction

Magnets attract other magnetic materials because they force the domains in magnetic materials to line up with their own domains. Before a material is magnetized, its domains are randomly arranged. When a magnet is brought near the material, all the domains face the same way. The magnet produces an opposite magnetic pole in the closest part of the material. So the north pole of the magnet will produce a south pole in the material it attracts.

The Story of the Compass

The invention of the compass came about by chance around the first century AD. It took another 1,000 years before people began to use compasses as tools to find their way around.

Sailors once used compasses such as this ship's compass to navigate on the open ocean.

Accidental Invention

In China, people found they could use lodestone to magnetize pieces of iron. They rubbed the iron with the rock to create the magnet. They noticed that the iron pieces aligned themselves in the same direction—pointing toward the North Pole. Without even realizing it, they had invented the compass.

How It Works

The compass works as a pointer to reference Earth's magnetic poles. Since the needle of the compass is made from a magnetic material, it aligns with Earth's magnetic field. The end of the needle seeking north points toward the magnetic north pole, and the other end points toward the magnetic south pole.

Compass Errors

Compasses are not entirely accurate. Map directions always use Earth's geographical North Pole as a reference point, but a compass references Earth's magnetic north pole. Since Earth's magnetic poles are not in exactly the same place as the geographical poles, using a compass can send you in the wrong direction. In addition, compass readings can be wrong near the magnetic poles due to variations in Earth's magnetic field.

Hikers often plot their courses using a compass and a map.

LIFE WITHOUT THE COMPASS

The compass has been a vital tool for getting around since the twelfth century. Chinese sailors used compasses to navigate on the open ocean. Even today, some people prefer compasses to modern GPS units because compasses do not rely on a power source.

23

Magnetic Alignment

All you need to do to make a magnet is to align the domains in the magnetic material in the same direction. There are four main ways you can do this.

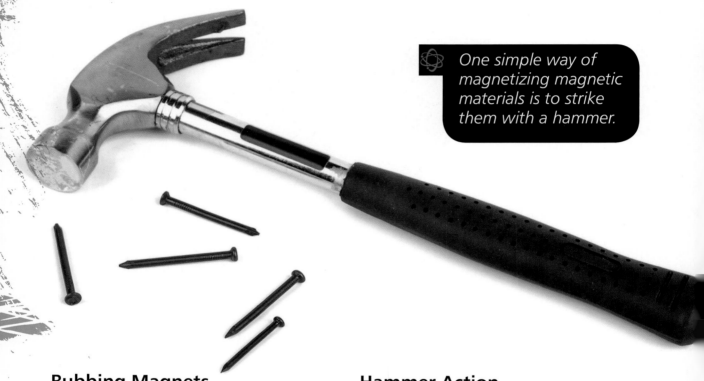

One simple way of magnetizing magnetic materials is to strike them with a hammer.

Rubbing Magnets

One of the easiest ways to magnetize a magnetic material is to stroke it with a magnet. Rubbing the material with the north or south poles of the magnet encourages the domains to line up. This is how people made the first magnets thousands of years ago.

Hammer Action

Another way of making magnets is to strike the magnetic material with a hammer. You can magnetize a piece of iron in this way by holding the iron in a north-south direction and then striking it repeatedly. The force of the blows knocks the magnetic domains in the iron out of their random arrangement. Eventually, the domains line up in a north-south direction.

Electric Power

Passing an electric current through a magnetic material also causes the domains to line up. This is how electromagnets are made (see Chapter Five). The strength of the electromagnet depends on how much electric current flows through the electromagnet, among other factors.

Force Field

A common way of making a magnet is to hold the magnetic material in a magnetic field. The field forces the domains in the material to line up along the north-south lines of the magnetic field.

SUPER SCIENCE FACT

There are two main ways to demagnetize a magnet. The most common method is to align the magnet in a magnetic field that is aligned in the opposite direction to the magnet. Another way is to heat the magnet above a certain critical temperature. Heat makes the domains drop out of alignment.

Chapter Four
Measuring Magnetism

As scientists began to understand how magnetism works, they invented machines to measure it. They also invented a system of standard units to measure magnetism and its effects.

How Much Magnetism?

When scientists began to study magnets, they found that some magnets were much stronger than others. They needed a way to measure the strength of magnetic fields and to study the effects of magnetism. So they invented many different machines, some of which are still used today.

Magnetometers

Scientists use a machine called a magnetometer to measure the strength of a magnet. Magnetometers are often called gaussmeters in honor of the German scientist Carl Friedrich Gauss. He invented the first magnetometer in 1833. Magnetometers can now be used to measure everything from small bar magnets to Earth's magnetic field.

This weighing device measures the strength of an electromagnet by the weight it can lift.

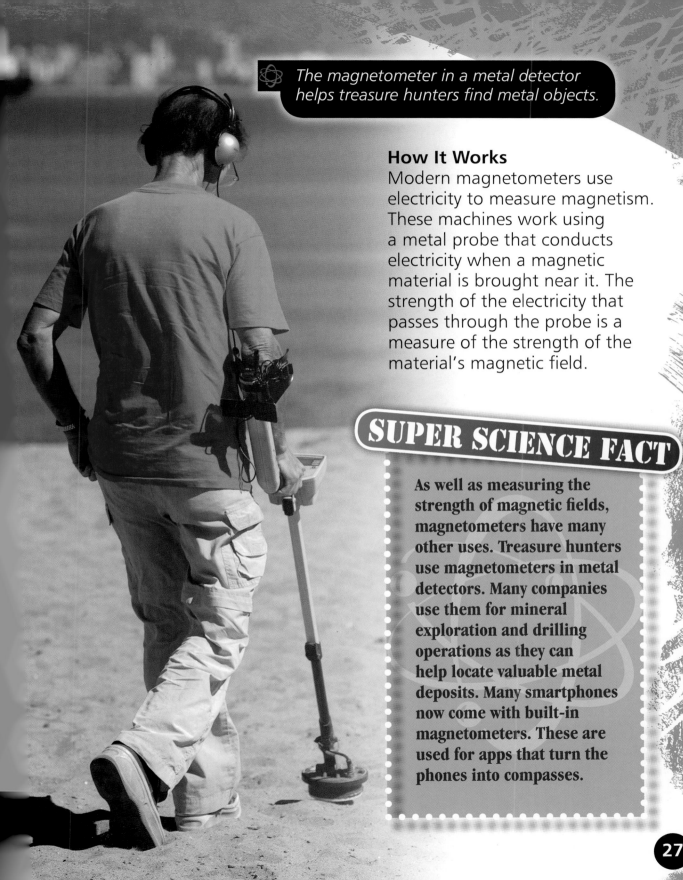

The magnetometer in a metal detector helps treasure hunters find metal objects.

How It Works

Modern magnetometers use electricity to measure magnetism. These machines work using a metal probe that conducts electricity when a magnetic material is brought near it. The strength of the electricity that passes through the probe is a measure of the strength of the material's magnetic field.

SUPER SCIENCE FACT

As well as measuring the strength of magnetic fields, magnetometers have many other uses. Treasure hunters use magnetometers in metal detectors. Many companies use them for mineral exploration and drilling operations as they can help locate valuable metal deposits. Many smartphones now come with built-in magnetometers. These are used for apps that turn the phones into compasses.

Magnetic Units

Scientists use special units to measure magnetism and its effects. Many of these units are named in honor of scientists who made important discoveries in this field of science.

Standard Units

It is important to have a standard system of units to measure and describe scientific things. Scientists work in different countries and speak different languages, so they need to work with common units to understand each other.

The Tesla

Scientists use the tesla (T) to measure the strength of a magnetic field. This unit is named in honor of Serbian-born scientist Nikola Tesla. Tesla did a lot of research in electricity and magnetism.

The Gauss

Teslas are useful for measuring large magnetic fields. Scientists use a unit called the gauss (G) to measure smaller magnetic fields. One tesla is equal to 10,000 gauss. To give you an idea of what this means, Earth's magnetic field measures about 0.5 gauss at the surface of the planet. Fridge magnets measure 100 gauss, while a strong electromagnet can measure 1,500 gauss.

Carl Gauss (pictured) worked with German scientist Wilhelm Weber to establish the units for magnetism.

 The magnetic field of a fridge magnet fixes the magnet to the fridge door.

Math Lesson

Scientists use complex mathematical equations to describe the behavior of magnets. These equations relate the units of magnetism to other units that you can measure. For example, the tesla is actually a measure of the density of the magnetic lines of force around a magnet. The magnetic lines of force are described in units called webers (Wb), which is a measure of the current flowing through a magnet. A magnetometer records the current and uses math to convert the measurement into teslas.

Chapter Five

Electromagnetism

Electricity is the movement of electrons through a conductor, such as a metal. Since many metals are magnetic materials, the movement of electrons also creates a magnetic field. Electricity and magnetism may seem like different things, but they are both part of the same force. This combined force is called electromagnetism.

A telecommunications tower picks up electromagnetic signals to connect people on the phone.

Understanding Electromagnetism

A Danish scientist named Hans Ørsted was the first person to make the connection between electricity and magnetism. In 1819, Ørsted was experimenting with electricity in his laboratory. He noticed that the needle of a nearby compass flickered whenever he flicked a switch to turn his equipment on and off. Ørsted realized that electricity flowing through the wires in the electrical equipment had created a magnetic field, which then attracted the compass needle. By accident, Ørsted had discovered electromagnetism.

Electromagnetic Effects

Other scientists tested Ørsted's discovery. They passed electricity through a single wire and found that the current passing through the wire created a magnetic field. When they turned off the electricity, the magnetic effect stopped.

Electromagnetism is one of the four fundamental forces of nature. The other forces are gravity, the strong nuclear force, and the weak nuclear force.

Faraday's Genius

English scientist and inventor Michael Faraday took this idea a step further. He realized that if electricity could create magnetism, then perhaps the effect would work the other way around. He moved a magnet near a wire and found that electricity flowed through it. Faraday realized that the magnetic field cutting through the wire had created an electrical current through the wire. This discovery was very important. Faraday had found a way to make electricity from the movement of a magnet. Today, most of the electricity in the world is made in this way.

Sir Michael Faraday was a brilliant scientist who figured out the laws of electromagnetic induction.

What Is an Electromagnet?

Since electricity creates magnetism, it is often used to make powerful magnets called electromagnets. These magnets work only when electricity flows through the magnetic material. When the electricity stops, the magnetic force stops.

The tightly wound coils of wire increase the strength of this electromagnet.

Electromagnets in Action

Most people have seen an electromagnet in action. Take a trip to the junkyard and you will see huge electromagnets moving cars, hauling the scrap vehicles into the air, and dropping them back down again.

Electromagnets Made Simple

Electromagnets are very simple. They consist of a core of metal, such as iron, around which is wrapped a length of conducting wire. When you connect a power source, electricity flows through the wire. The movement of electrons through the wire creates a magnetic field around the wire. This magnetizes the iron core inside the wire.

On and Off

One of the most useful things about an electromagnet is that you can turn it on and off. Electricity must flow through the wire to magnetize the iron core. As soon as you turn off the power supply, the magnetic field disappears. In this way, you can switch on an electromagnet to pick up a car in a junkyard and then switch the electromagnet off when you want to drop it elsewhere.

SUPER SCIENCE FACT

Electromagnets are found in many different devices, ranging from computer hard drives to loudspeakers (see Chapter Six). Even your doorbell is powered by an electromagnet. Pressing the doorbell completes an electric circuit. The electricity then creates a magnetic field that magnetizes the ringer. The bell attracts the ringer, which hits the bell to make it chime.

A doorbell makes use of electromagnetism to chime a bell and make a sound.

Sticking Power

When scientists discovered electromagnetism, they tried to make stronger electromagnets. They found that the magnetic field increased when they wrapped the wire into tight coils around a core of a magnetic metal such as iron.

Electromagnets are a common part of many modern electrical devices.

Homemade Electromagnet
You can make an electromagnet at home using a battery, a nail, and a length of fuse wire. All you need to do is wrap the wire around the nail, and connect each end to the battery. It is best to use insulated wire because the wire gets hot when electricity flows through it.

Loop the Loop
A homemade electromagnet does not create a very strong magnetic field. Scientists have found ways to make them stronger. One of the main things that determines the strength of an electromagnet is the number of times you wrap the wire around the metal core. This coiled wire is called a solenoid. Using more coils makes a stronger electromagnet.

Magnetic Core

The strength of an electromagnet also depends on what material you use for the solenoid. Materials that support the formation of magnetic fields are called permeable materials. An iron nail is a good choice for your homemade electromagnet because it is a naturally magnetic and highly permeable material.

SUPER SCIENCE FACT

Wrapping a wire more tightly around a solenoid makes a much stronger electromagnet. It increases the number of loops in the coil, which increases the electric current that flows around the solenoid. In turn, this makes the electromagnet stronger.

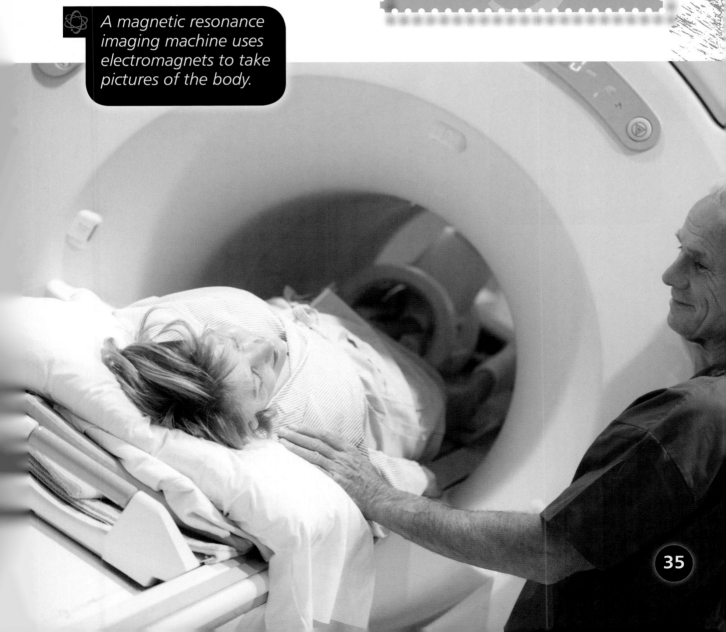

A magnetic resonance imaging machine uses electromagnets to take pictures of the body.

Power Up

Any source of electricity can be used to power an electromagnet. You can create your own electromagnet at home or in the science lab using the power from a battery. On an industrial scale, the electricity may come from a large generator at a power station.

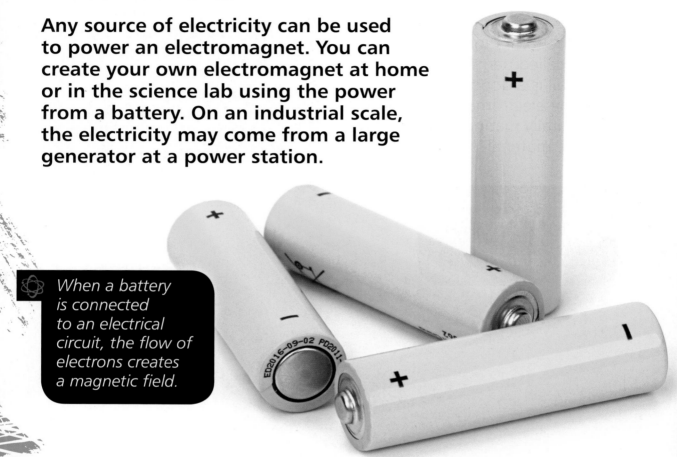

When a battery is connected to an electrical circuit, the flow of electrons creates a magnetic field.

Source of Power

A battery is simply a source of electrons that can be used to create an electric current. It has two terminals—a positive terminal and a negative terminal. When a battery is disconnected, the electrons gather at the negative terminal of the battery. These electrons are released during a chemical reaction that takes place inside the battery. When you connect the battery to a wire around a solenoid, you complete an electric circuit. The electrons at the negative terminal can flow through the wire to the positive terminal. This flow of electrons is the electricity that creates a magnetic field.

Some people think that electromagnetism creates Earth's magnetic field. Deep beneath Earth's surface lies a core of molten iron, which means the iron is so hot it has turned to liquid. The swirling mass of liquid iron generates an electric current, which creates the magnetic field around our planet. This is known as the dynamo effect.

Industrial Electromagnets

Batteries cannot produce enough electricity to power an industrial electromagnet. Generators are used instead. A generator is a machine that makes electricity using magnetism. The magnets inside a generator produce electricity. This electricity feeds into the wire coil of the electromagnet, which magnetizes the solenoid inside the coil to make a much stronger electromagnet.

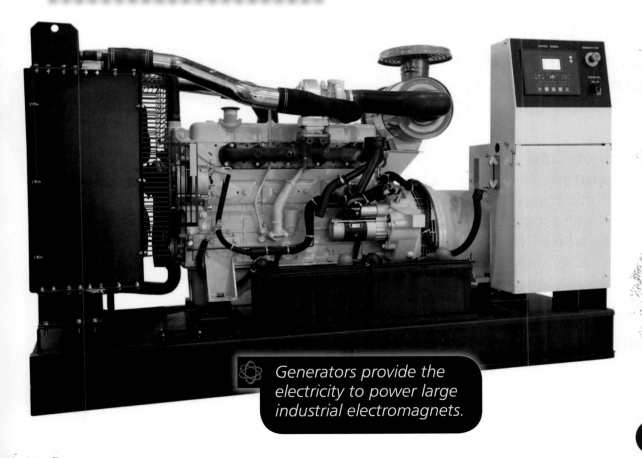

Generators provide the electricity to power large industrial electromagnets.

Chapter Six

Electromagnets in Action

Electromagnets have many uses in everyday life, from computers and electric motors to loudspeakers and television sets. Electromagnets are useful because you can control the magnetic field simply by switching the power on and off.

Magnets and Computers

Electronic computers have been around only since the middle of the twentieth century, but they are an essential part of many people's lives. People use computers every day—for surfing the Internet, playing games, and sending emails.

Information Store

Computers use electromagnets to store information. A computer processes information as pulses of electricity. A pulse of electricity is stored as a "1" and no pulse is stored as a "0."

Computer hard drives use electromagnets to store binary data—sequences of 0s and 1s that represent electricity turning off and on.

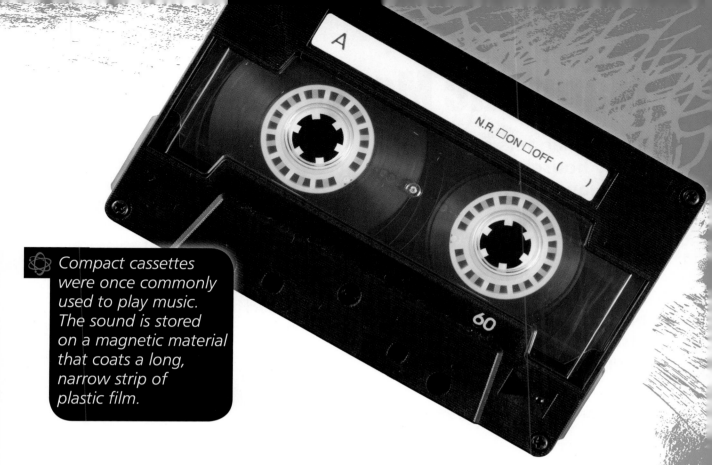

Compact cassettes were once commonly used to play music. The sound is stored on a magnetic material that coats a long, narrow strip of plastic film.

When you save a file on a computer, the 0s and 1s are stored on a magnetic hard drive. An electromagnet lines up the magnetic poles to represent the 0s and 1s. The electromagnet is also used to read the information stored on the hard drive.

Magnets for Movement

Motors power all the moving parts of a computer, from the fans that cool the processor to stop it from overheating to the hard drive that spins at high speed as it stores information. These motors contain magnets that convert electricity into movement (see pages 40–41).

LIFE WITHOUT COMPUTERS

Imagine a world without computers. People use PCs, laptops, and tablets all the time at school, in the office, and at home. Computers also control most electronic machines and the engines of vehicles such as cars and trains. Computers make our lives much easier, but some people think we rely on them too much.

Magnetic Movement

Electromagnets control many household appliances, from lawn mowers and sewing machines to microwave ovens and washing machines. Powerful electromagnets are also used to power electric vehicles such as streetcars, trains, and even modern automobiles.

What Is a Motor?

A motor is a machine that uses electricity to make things move. British scientist Michael Faraday made the first electric motor in 1821. He discovered that a vertically mounted wire carrying an electric current would rotate around a magnet sticking out of a bowl of mercury.

The alternator of a car uses electromagnets to generate power for electrical parts, such as the headlights and the instrument panel.

How It Works

The motor works because electricity creates a magnetic field as it flows through the wire coil. The coil spins because its magnetic field pushes against the magnetic field of the magnet. This magnetic push is the driving force of the electric motor.

Modern Motors

Faraday's first motor was very simple. It did not have enough power to work a machine. Over time, inventors improved Faraday's design. The first improvement was adding a commutator to the coil. This changed the direction of the electric current at every half turn of the coil to keep it spinning. They also found that increasing the number of turns in the coil increased the magnetic field around the coil, which made the motor more powerful.

A washing machine uses an electric motor to rotate the drum as it washes the clothes.

SUPER SCIENCE FACT

The engines of most modern cars burn gasoline for power. This creates harmful gases that pollute the atmosphere and contribute to global warming. Many people think that electric-powered vehicles will solve this problem. But these vehicles need electricity for power, and the electricity comes from burning fossil fuels.

Particle Accelerators

Some of the most powerful electromagnets in the world are used to power machines called particle accelerators. Scientists are using these massive complex machines to unlock the secrets of the universe.

Atom Smashers

Particle accelerators use powerful electromagnets to accelerate the particles found inside atoms to speeds approaching the speed of light, and then smash them to pieces. Scientists study the collisions to investigate energy and matter, and the forces that hold the particles together.

These are parts from a particle accelerator. Particle accelerators are sometimes called "atom smashers."

Riding the Wave

Particle accelerators work by speeding up particles on a "wave" of electromagnetic radiation. The electromagnets inside the machine switch on and off rapidly. The pulses of electricity speed up the particles to the speed of light, and the magnetic field keeps the beam of particles on target.

Massive Machines

There are two main types of particle accelerator: linear accelerators and circular accelerators. In linear accelerators, the particles travel down a straight tunnel and then collide with the target. The Stanford Linear Accelerator in California is the world's longest linear accelerator. It is 1.8 miles (3 km) long. In circular accelerators, the particles travel around in a huge circle before smashing into the target. The Fermilab Tevatron is the world's largest circular accelerator. It is 4 miles (6.4 km) long.

The particle accelerators at the European Organization for Nuclear Research (CERN) in Switzerland use some of the most powerful magnets in the world.

Magnetism for the Future

Magnets play an important part in our world, helping people do many tasks much more quickly and easily. Just think of all the machines in your home that use magnets in some way. Scientists and inventors are coming up with new and exciting ways to take advantage of this mysterious force of nature.

Nanomagnets

Scientists are developing incredibly small magnets that are only the size of atoms. These so-called "nanomagnets" are being used to make extremely small machines, or "nanomachines." One of the main uses of nanomachines is in medicine. Doctors hope to use nanomachines to treat cancer and other diseases.

Floating Trains

Magnetism is used to power high-speed trains. These trains do not have wheels but "float" on a magnetic field created by powerful electromagnets. The electromagnets switch on and off to propel the trains forward at hundreds of miles an hour. The trains are called maglev trains, which is short for magnetic levitation.

Magnetic Slingshot

Scientists are investigating magnetism as a means to launch satellites into space. They imagine the satellites racing around a giant circular track leading to a ramp. Powerful electromagnets could accelerate the satellites up to 14,400 miles (23,000 km) per hour, which is fast enough to escape Earth's gravity and slingshot them into space. The rockets that launch satellites and other spacecraft into space can be used just once. One of the advantages of the magnetic ramp is that it could be used again and again.

Scientists hope they can launch spacecraft into space using powerful electromagnets rather than rockets.

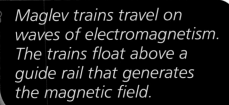

Maglev trains travel on waves of electromagnetism. The trains float above a guide rail that generates the magnetic field.

SUPER SCIENCE FACT

Scottish scientist James Clerk Maxwell used complex math to link the forces of electricity and magnetism in 1861. Today, scientists are working on a "Grand Unified Theory" to link all the fundamental forces, such as gravity and the forces that hold atoms together. They hope this theory might provide a clue about how the universe was created.

45

Glossary

alloy a mixture of metals

atoms the tiny particles that make up everything in the universe

auroras shimmering bands of light in the night sky, common around the North and South Poles

battery a source of electricity consisting of one or more electric cells

compass an instrument that shows direction. The needle of a compass is a magnet that points toward Earth's magnetic north pole.

conduct to allow electricity to flow through easily

electricity the flow of electrons through an object

electromagnetic radiation energy that flows through space as particles and waves

electromagnetism magnetism created by a current of electricity

electron a tiny particle found inside an atom. Electrons carry negative electric charge.

force the push or pull on an object to make it move

generator a machine that converts movement into electricity

gravity the force of attraction between objects

lodestone a naturally occurring magnetic rock containing the iron ore magnetite

magnetic field the space around a magnet in which the magnet can attract other magnetic materials

metal a solid substance that is usually hard, shiny, and a good conductor of electricity

motor a machine that converts electricity into movement

neutron a tiny particle found inside the nucleus of an atom. Neutrons carry no electric charge.

nucleus the center of an atom, which contains protons and neutrons

orbital the curved path of an electron around the nucleus of an atom

particle accelerator a machine that uses electromagnets to accelerate tiny particles at speeds approaching the speed of light

permeable able to be moved through

pole one of the two ends of a magnet—one is the north pole and one is the south pole

pollute to release harmful substances into the environment

proton a tiny particle found inside the nucleus of an atom. Protons carry positive electric charge.

solenoid a coil of wire that acts as a magnet when an electric current flows through it

For More Information

Books

Hartman, Eve, and Meshbesher, Wendy. *Magnetism and Electromagnets*. North Mankato, MN: Heinemann-Raintree, 2009.

Lachner, Elizabeth. *Magnetic Forces*. New York, NY: Powerkids Press, 2009.

Swanson, Jennifer, and Bernice Lum. *The Attractive Truth about Magnetism*. North Mankato, MN: Capstone Press, 2012.

Taylor-Butler, Christine. *Experiments with Magnets and Metals*. North Mankato, MN: Heinemann-Raintree, 2011.

Websites

What do a junkyard, a rock concert, and your front door have in common? Find out the answer at:
www.howstuffworks.com/electromagnet.htm

Watch two industrial scientists, Richard Ambrose and Jonny Phillips, explain the science behind magnets at:
video.nationalgeographic.co.uk/video/kids/cartoons-tv-movies-kids/i-didnt-know-that-kids/idkt-magnets-kids

Publisher's note to educators and parents: Our editors have carefully reviewed these websites to ensure that they are suitable for students. Many websites change frequently, however, and we cannot guarantee that a site's future contents will continue to meet our high standards of quality and educational value. Be advised that students should be closely supervised whenever they access the Internet.

Index